I Had A Brother

by Joanne Parker

Illustrated by Sarah Posey

Wyatt House Publishing

Mobile, Alabama
www.wyattpublishing.com

© Copyright 2019- Joanne Parker

All rights reserved. Permission is granted to copy or reprint portions for any noncommercial use, except they may not be posted online without permission.

Wyatt House books may be ordered through booksellers or by contacting:

WYATT HOUSE PUBLISHING
399 Lakeview Dr. W.
Mobile, Alabama 36695
www.wyattpublishing.com
editor@wyattpublishing.com

Because of the dynamic nature of the Internet, any web address or links contained in this book may have changed since publication and may no longer be valid.

Cover and interior design by: Mark Wyatt

ISBN 13: 978-0-9896119-8-5

Printed in the United States of America

For My Family

I had a brother. He was smart and kind. He could run really fast. He could tell a joke and make everything better.

We shared bunk beds. We played army and games and rode bikes together. We told each other scary stories and rolled our eyes at each other when we were told to stop burping at the table.

We rode the bus together to school. We sat in the way, way back of the car on road trips. We dreamed of having the power of Superman and we built forts and captured pirates all day.

As we got older we collected baseball cards and we carved each other's numbers in the dirt with our cleats for good luck. We stayed up for hours defending our virtual kingdoms and playing video games until our fingers hurt.

But one day an accident happened and now he's gone. Dad told me he was in heaven and we didn't have to be sad. Mom told me we could remember the good times we had with him. Grandad said he was special and loved.

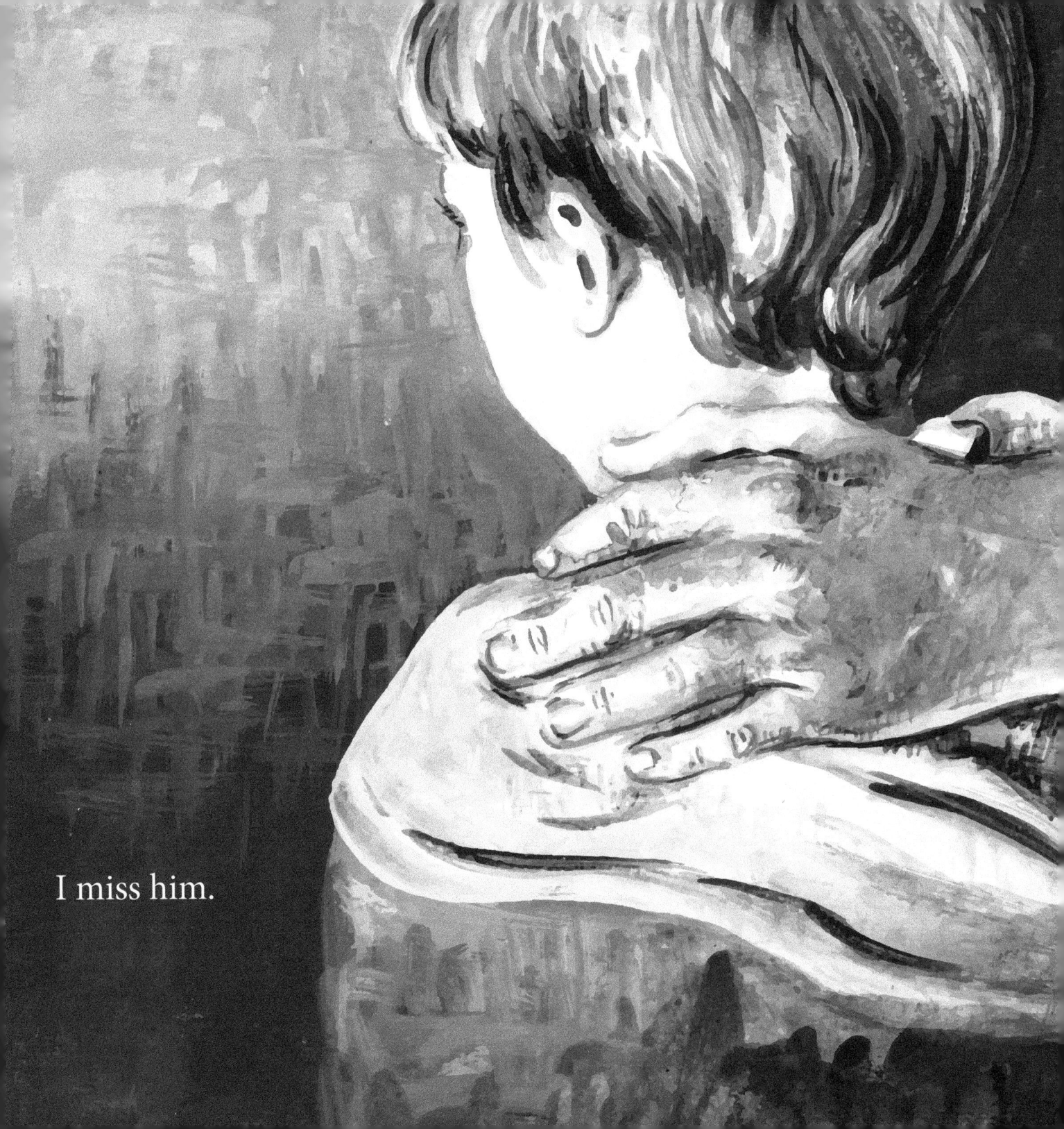

I miss him.

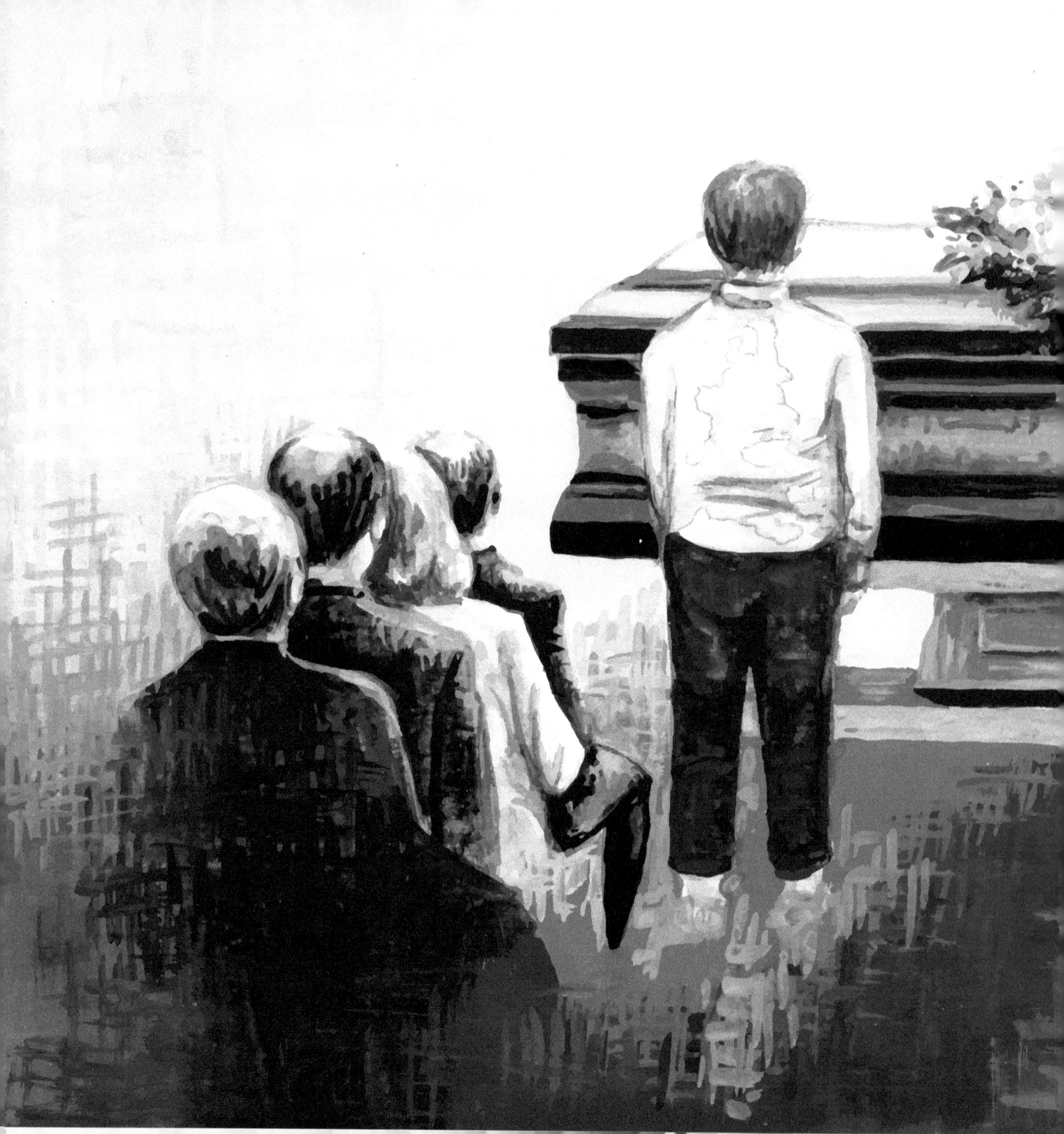

Everyone was quiet at the funeral home and there was a lot of crying. I wished he had been there to make it stop hurting. Everyone was quiet by his casket and there was a lot of hugging. I wished heaven would give him back.

I miss him.

I miss playing baseball with my brother. I miss having someone to play superheroes with. I miss having someone to build forts with.

I miss standing on my tiptoes to see who measures taller against the door frame in the hall.

I miss him.

And I need to keep playing sports because he would. And I need to keep laughing and telling jokes because he would. And I need to keep fighting the bad guys because he would. And I need to keep growing and learning and smiling because he would.

...even though I miss him.

Today we went to visit the grave. Mom hugged me and said we could visit anytime.

8 37

I carved our numbers in the dirt with a stick. It's not always easy to talk about him without crying so I talked to him today at the grave.

Today we went to the park. We played all day in the sunshine. He would have really liked that. I felt like he was smiling down on me from heaven.

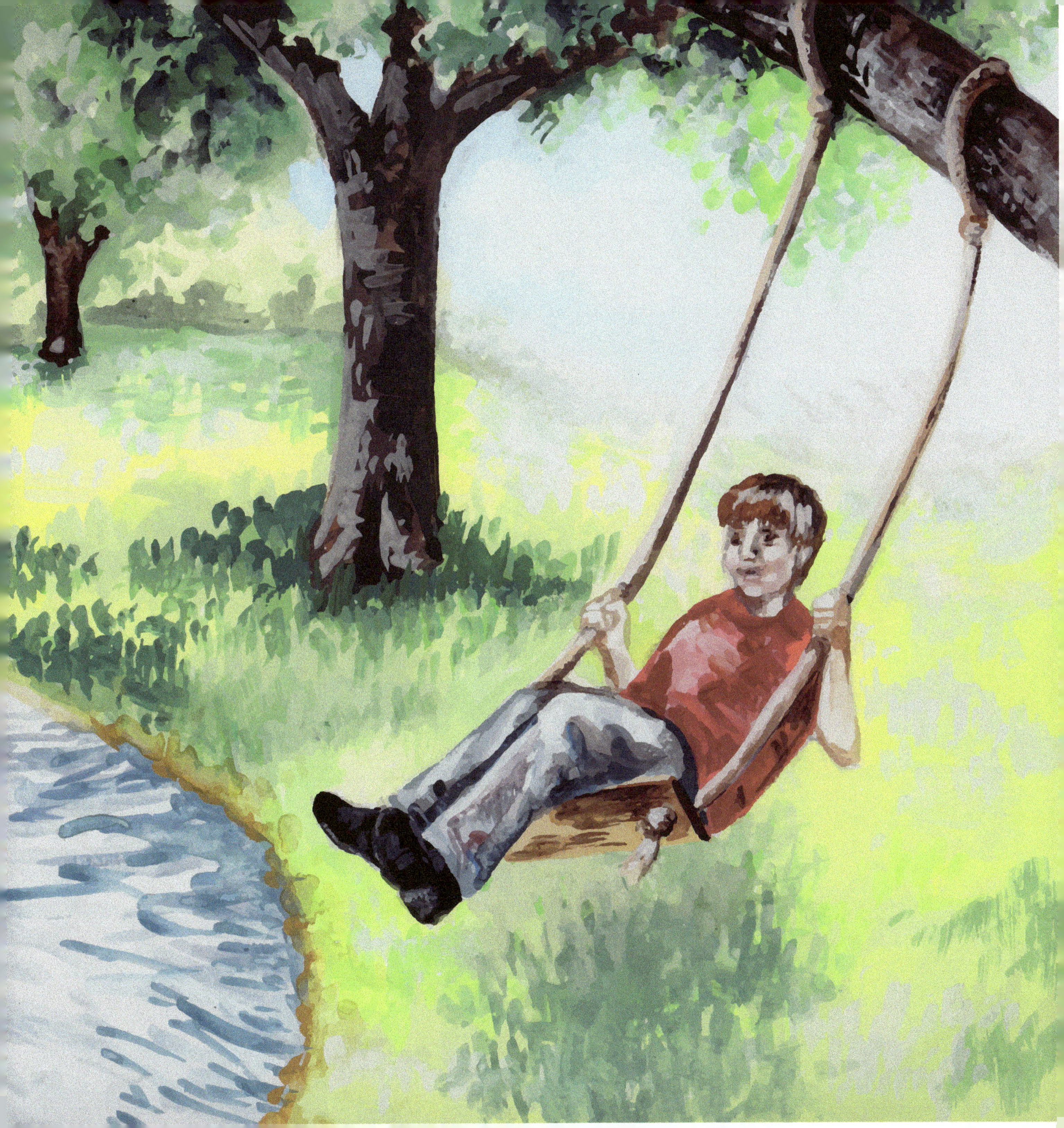

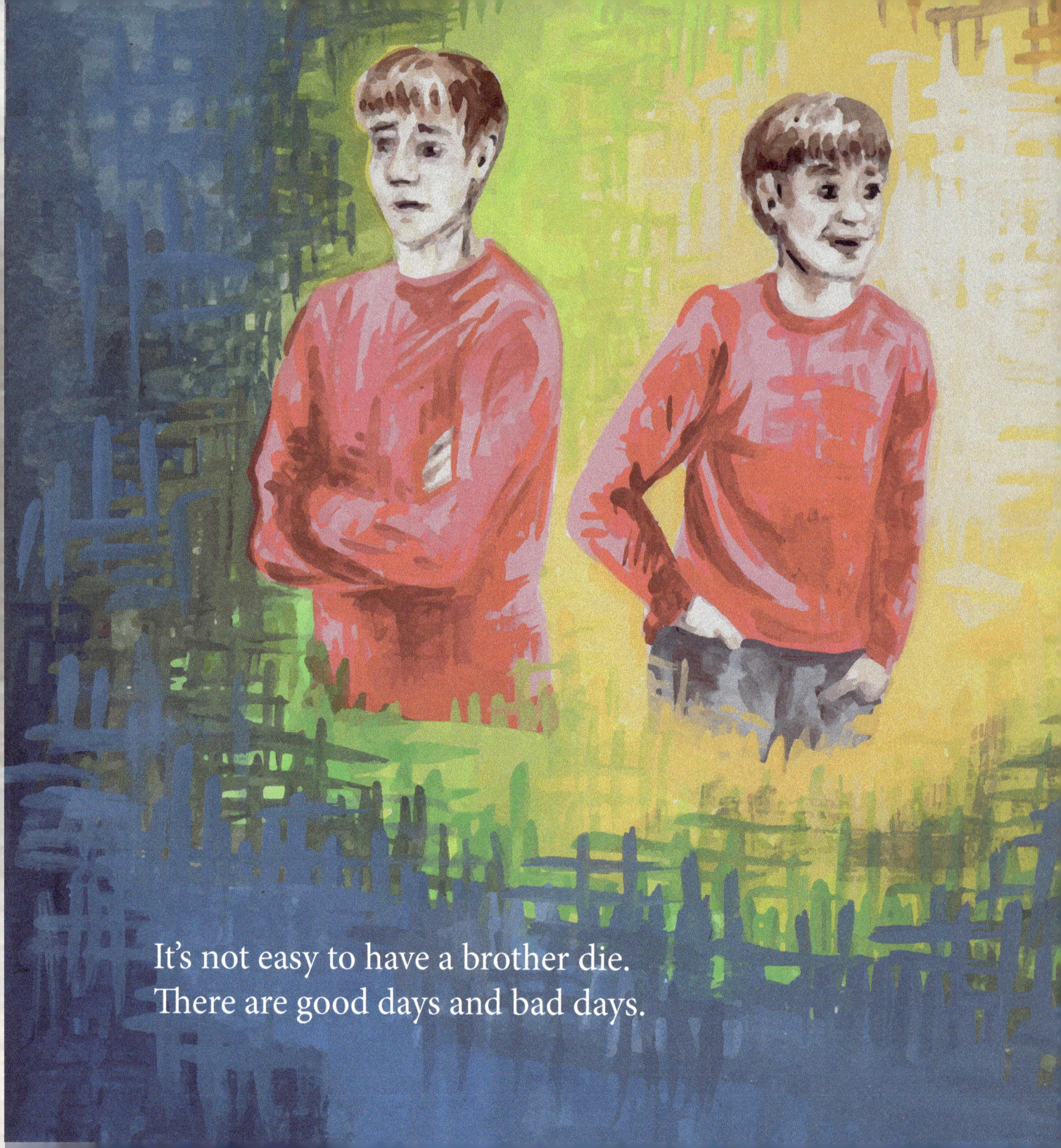

It's not easy to have a brother die.
There are good days and bad days.

There are times I remember him and laugh.
There are times I remember him and cry.

It's nice to know he's not hurting or scared. It makes me happy to know I'll see him again.

I had a brother. He was strong and brave and kind. And today, I'll be strong and brave and kind as I remember him and smile.

Other Resources:

Bereavedparentsusa.org

Compassionatefriends.org

Umbrellaministries.com

Remembering My Someone Special, Grieving Journal for Kids
(www.christianbook.com)

BASIS
(HVMI.org)

Joanneparkerbooks.com

Joanne Parker is a writer from West Chester, PA. After the death of her sister following a fatal car accident she decided to write a book about grief and loss to offer people hope and healing. Her first book was *I Had a Sister*. When she's not running after one of her four children, she keeps herself busy with music, theater, CrossFit, and local volunteering. She currently lives in Mobile, AL with her family and two dogs.

Sarah Posey is a freelance painter from Mobile, Alabama, currently pursuing an undergraduate degree in painting from the Savannah College of Art and Design. Besides illustrating *I Had a Sister* and *I Had a Brother*, Sarah has dabbled in commissioned portraiture, graphic design, and has been shown in several local and regional fine art shows.

You have a story.
We want to publish it.

Everyone has as a story to tell. It might be about something you know how to do, or what has happened in your life, or it may be a thrilling, or romantic, or intriguing, or heartwarming, or suspenseful story, starring a cast of characters that have been swimming around in your imagination.

And at Wyatt House Publishing, we can get your story onto the pages of a book just like the one you are holding in your hand. With professional interior design and a custom, professionally designed cover built just for you from the start, you can finally see your dream of being an author become reality. Then, you will see your book listed with retailers all over the world as people are able to buy your book from wherever they are and have it delivered to their home or their e-reader.

So what are you waiting for? This is your time.

visit us at
www.wyattpublishing.com

for details on how to get started becoming a published author right away.

CPSIA information can be obtained
at www.ICGtesting.com
Printed in the USA
LVHW072015180120
644131LV00003B/6